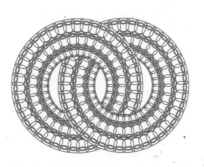

ALL AT ONCE

ALL AT ONCE

JACK RIDL

CAVANKERRY
PRESS

CavanKerry Press Ltd.
Fort Lee, New Jersey
www.cavankerrypress.org

Publisher's Cataloging-in-Publication Data
provided by Five Rainbows Cataloging Services
Names: Ridl, Jack, author.
Title: All at once / Jack Ridl.
Description: Fort Lee, NJ : CavanKerry Press, 2024.
Identifiers: ISBN 978-1-960327-06-2 (paperback)
Subjects: LCSH: Michigan—Poetry. | Spirituality—Poetry. | Nature—
    Poetry. | Families—Poetry. | Sports—Poetry. | Psychic trauma—
    Poetry. | BISAC: POETRY / Subjects & Themes / Family. | POETRY /
    Subjects & Themes / Inspirational & Religious. | SELF-HELP /
    Creativity.
Classification: LCC PS3618.I35 A44 2024 (print) | DDC 811/.6—dc23.

Cover photo "One Day" Original Acrylic & Pencil Painting on Panel
    Box, courtesy of Artist Meridith Ridl. Represented by LaFontsee
    Galleries.
Cover and interior text design by Ryan Scheife, Mayfly Design
First Edition 2024, Printed in the United States of America

CavanKerry Press is proud to publish the works of established poets
of merit and distinction.

Made possible by funds from the
New Jersey State Council on the Arts, a partner
agency of the National Endowment for the Arts.

CavanKerry Press is grateful for the support it receives from the
New Jersey State Council on the Arts.

In addition, CavanKerry Press gratefully acknowledges generous
emergency support received during the COVID-19 pandemic from
the following funders:

The Academy of American Poets

Community of Literary Magazines and Presses

National Book Foundation

New Jersey Arts and Culture Recovery Fund

New Jersey Council for the Humanities

New Jersey Economic Development Authority

Northern New Jersey Community Foundation

The Poetry Foundation

US Small Business Administration

Also by Jack Ridl

The Same Ghost (1984)

Between (1988)

Poems from The Same Ghost and Between (1993)

Approaching Poetry (with Peter Schakel, 1997)

Against Elegies (2001)

250 Poems: A Portable Anthology (with Peter Schakel, 2003)

Approaching Literature in the 21st Century
    (with Peter Schakel, 2005)

Broken Symmetry (2006)

Losing Season (2009)

Practicing to Walk Like A Heron (2013)

Saint Peter and the Goldfinch (2019)

For Julie who keeps my heart, and keeps my heart in it.
For Meridith, loving daughter, my light.
For Betsy, my sister, always there.

Thought without emotion is unredeemed.
– Richard Jones

What I wanted was inclusion, to be connected.
– D.R. James

I can think these words to the page—just for you—
but don't know if they make any sense.
– Dan Gerber

"Daddy, 'with' is the most important word in the world
because we are always 'with.'"
– Meridith Ridl, age 7

Contents

All at Once   1

I. Caught in the Web

Today Our Daughter, a Teacher, Wasn't Shot   5
Christmas, 1943   7
Caught in the Web   9
My Mother's Week   10
Mud and Dust   11
Ten Inches of Snow Overnight   12
Recovery   13
I Have No Idea Why This Is Just to Say   14
It Could Be   15
Waiting for Covid   16
What If   17
Across the Room   21

II. One Childhood

Let Us Break Bread Together on Our Knees   25
It's Always Within the Wood   26
I Thought About Putting Together a Jigsaw Puzzle   27
How We Must Waken   28
Mid-Morning   29
One Childhood   30
Once It Happens   31
Clothespins   33

Bartholomew: Disciple   34
A Perfect Day for a Ballgame   36
On Certain Nights   37
Because of William Stafford   38

III. The Lost Similes

The New Normal   41
"If It Didn't Exist, I Wouldn't Miss It"   42
After Reading the Table of Contents of Three Literary
    Magazines and Recognizing Two Names   43
My Mother's Ivory Hippopotamus   44
Saint Mark and His Piano   45
Have You Had Your Vaccine?   46
Maybe Tomorrow   48
The Man Who Loved Olives   50
How It Should Be   51
What? You Wouldn't Want to Be a Dog?   52
The Lost Similes   53

IV. Some Kid Was Shot

Just Before Spring   57
On the Inhumane Hideaway of Objective Distance   58
The Night Before a Friend Had to Put Down Her Dog   60
Grief Again   62
Remember That Rock Song?   63
Her Bed   64
On the Bus to Poland   66
He Had to Put It Off for a Year   68
Yesterday I Buried a Female Cardinal   69
Light at the End of Day   70
There's Been a Suicide on This Page   71
On Another Anniversary of My Father's Death   72

V. The Worth of Waiting

Margaritaville Farewell   75
After Leaving Bed at 2 AM I Wondered If I was Still in the
    Same House   76
Nathaniel Before the Storm   77
At Home   78
Before What Came Before   79
The One Note   80
High Fly: The Outfielder   81
The Hidden Permutations of Love   82
The Worth of Waiting   83
All I Know Is It Was Dark   84

Acknowledgments   87

All at Once

That's how it happens. Always
happens. It could be at a circus,
the clowns all smiling beneath

their paint. They could point
their plastic guns and fire,
filling the stands with popcorn. Maybe

we would laugh like we used to
when no eighteen-year-old
would thoughtfully consider

firing round after round from
a semi-automatic birthday present
into the waiting stares from

bodies unwillingly growing
day by day into those same teen
years. There alone stood

Tigger, while Pooh,
Piglet, Christopher Robin,
and Eeyore lived on for another

day. Those too young to understand
were read to until sleep came again
in the middle of a chapter. It's always

too late to turn the page. There
they all stood, taking shot after
shot. Then they weren't

home on time where someone
was making dinner, playing Hearts
or Uno, watching Wheel of Fortune.

That morning everyone woke with two
days until summer break. Two more
school lunch hours, maybe three or

four more words to learn to spell,
maybe the last chapter of *Little House*,
sure that in just two days, they

would all walk out together saying,
"See ya at the pool," "at the playground,"
"at your place." "See ya next year."

I.

CAUGHT IN THE WEB

Today Our Daughter, a Teacher, Wasn't Shot

This afternoon another school massacre.
Since January more mass murders than
the year has days. In Grandmother's

attic, my father hid the rifle
he carried through Belgium, France,
and the snake-tangled vines of the

Philippines. While he led his men, my
grandmother smoked Pall Malls and
mothered my mother carrying me

toward a birth, while upstairs her husband,
my mother's father, the man I would
be named for and never know, lay

dying, penicillin hiding in a petri dish
revealing itself too late to keep him
here, to rockabye his grandson. Forty

years before, my grandmother, a five-year-old
nurtured in the north of England, Penrith,
along the Scottish border, played

in privilege on the family estate, lost everything
all at once, to the king, her father killed,
thrown from his horse on "the hunt."

Her mother disappeared into a glazed-over
stare, lived without time in a cottage, and
sent the four young sisters to

the safety of the States. Under her Aunt Lil's roof,
and stiff upper lip, she became a young
woman giving way to the war, tuberculosis,

an inner-empty daughter. Ah, but she never
missed her cup of tea. Always
at four. The war went on. Her husband

died. I was born. The nurse brought me
in a blanket to my mother who said,
"I will never hold him." I learned later

why her words would matter. The war
ended. My father returned. We moved to
an even smaller town. Today, my wife

and I planted perennials, planted them
in a haphazard pattern throughout our
cottage garden. I imagined my mother

sitting by my grandmother's living
room window, waiting, the radio on.
And I will remember my grandmother's

lap, what it's like to be held.
After school our daughter will
stop by. We will hug.

Christmas, 1943

When my mother and father
married on a weekend pass,
my mother moved in

with her parents. My father leaving for
Europe, leading a Black Company: war
janitors gathering and hoisting debris—useless

rifles, broken down jeeps, shattered
helmets, scattered body parts stuffed
into canvas bags. They tossed it all onto

the beds of Army green dump trucks.
At home my mother carried me in her
uncelebrated womb. Upstairs her mother

field nursed her husband polluted with
tuberculosis. He sang all their songs:
"Your Feet's Too Big," "Polka Dots and

Moonbeams." My mother and her mother
often joined him. He died two weeks
before Christmas. I was born four months

later, became a parenthesis to their mourning.
They placed his name with me. Her womb,
the closest she ever held me. I

feel my grandmother's lap. She sat by
a window behind her small, scarred,
antique fold-down table with her cup of

tea, pack of Pall Malls, and her rippled
deck of cards for a day of Solitaire. She
and my mother listened to the waist-high

Philco: news from the front, swing music,
Jack Benny. Each morning Gram held me on
her lap, asked me what I wanted for Christmas.

Caught in the Web

Time and again it's been written—father
and son playing catch. Toss. Catch. Throw

hard. Catch in the web. Toss. Reach for
and catch a high, hard one. Catch in the

web. We're in the backyard, my father
and I playing catch, the only way

we talked. Every important
decision within the rest of my life

flew there between us, carried by the ball, its
stitches twirling indefinitely toward me, my

glove, the web. Each of his throws held a comma,
a question mark, at times an exclamation point.

There I learned that only if my arm's release
was luckily precise could a period appear

at the end of ambiguous demands. He never said
a word about God, politics, sex, what lay ahead.

The answers were where I caught them in the web.

My Mother's Week

Monday, washday. Tuesday, ironing.
Wednesday, bills. Thursday, dust and

clean the bathrooms. Friday, wash the windows,
windowsills. Saturday, groceries. Sunday, church,

set out the trash. And every day: letters
written, knit, sew, patch, empty

the refrigerator. Ironing day holds me
still. She ironed everything: shirts, sheets,

napkins, underwear, slips, socks, kitchen towels,
handkerchiefs. I remember her leaning over

the tapered board unfolded from its closet,
the iron spitting steam. Stroke, stroke, flip.

Repeat. Fold or hang. Last, the rags
to clean the car, dust, and wipe down any

grime. Work? Ritual? Labor? Secular? Sacred?
An ever present prayer? The television was

always on: *Queen for a Day, Merv Griffin,
The Price Is Right*. I never heard her sing.

And always my attentive, careful fear of the scorch.

Mud and Dust

That's where my pal lived. Upstairs
two bedrooms faced each other,
three beds in one, one big bed

in the other, and at the end
of the hallway, the bathroom:
clawfoot tub with a hose attached

to a shower head, a pink plastic
curtain his sisters always pulled
for "Privacy, Stupid! Don't you

go opening it." When anyone came
in from the rain, they left their shoes
on the mud-caked rug just inside

the back door. Hot summer days
turned the world to dust, a light
brown coating covering the pick-up

and the front porch where in a lidded
bucket were kept the endless
usefulness of rags. Their father, a man

made of stone, after dinner sat
on the porch, looked across the patch
of garden clustered with black-eyed Susans.

He never said a thing, then went to bed.

Ten Inches of Snow Overnight

Again, I see myself walking back and
forth in the psych ward. God didn't

know I was there. The doors were locked.
I had a window so I could watch the visitors

scraping the snow from their cars then
pull out and head home, maybe have

something to drink, have a show to watch,
fall asleep. Even if they had an answer,

no one dared to talk about me. I now
sleep beside my wife of forty years and with

our dog and two cats, foundlings huddled
behind the church's air conditioner, the kittens

maybe three weeks old. Every day
she offered them a formula to lick from

her fingers. One morning my therapist stared hard
into my eyes, then fiercely said, "You're an orphan,

have always been an orphan." I stared at her.
Back in my room I lay down, fell into sleep.

Recovery

It was too many years after the shock
to even care what chapter and verse

it was that opened up the innocent synapses
into trauma that now without a sign erupts

when least expected. Why would frying
eggs or driving past a deer decaying by the road

pull the trigger, pull it every time for thirty
years? Why? Because hellfire is ubiquitous to

the evangelical, the literal, the certain, many
of the sentences that Paul or Graham or Calvin wrote.

Like a mugging in an alley, each word
bloodied me, slammed me into catatonic

meditation. After seven wards, 13 electro-shocks,
multiple meds and therapists, my wife's accepting eye,

each trauma evaporated like my
father's lack of answers, my mother's numb disinterest.

Now I lug a bin of bird seed, spade, flat
of Dusty Miller, stuff my weathered

garden gloves in my jeans' back pocket, slap on the old
ball cap and head out back to fill the feeders, find

that place I'd overlooked, push aside the mulch and dig.

I Have No Idea Why This Is Just To Say

I was in bed, with five books stacked alongside
and our village's weekly newspaper. It was 9 pm,
easily a couple hours before sleep took me. I

thought I'd finish up the paper; you know, get it
out of the way before savoring the new collection
of poems, before moving on in the memoir, and

getting close to the middle of the three novels.
But the paper obligated me with its ten letters
from townspeople, a long article about the needs

of the school, why I should vote for the millage
increase required to build a new library to keep
up with the 21st century claims on all of us.

There was a profile of a local candidate for
state office, an article about seniors also needing
an increased millage to sustain them: lots

more seniors than in the past—us.
My own arthritis, after all, is molding me, merging
into my peripheral neuropathy.

And I tilt my head to read. I'm pretty sure
I can keep our gardens rising, blooming, but
one never knows. I love to read on the porch

(it overlooks the flowers and tomato vines),
and watch the birds, and snarl when some car has
no reason to roar by. My wife had fallen asleep.

It won't be long until the leaves begin to wilt.
Why am I telling you this? I'm not sure. Somehow
it seemed important, like I needed for you to know.

It Could Be

On the last day of the world (a Tuesday)
I'm sitting on an old Adirondack during
a deluge of a thunderstorm. A car drives

by, the water on the street splashing
with each revolution of its tires. The world
too is turning. I know that. It always has.

No slower, no more immediate today.
It's common as air to see an angel perched
up on the corner street light. She—it is she—

lets the rain soak into her lucent skin.
Yes, she's naked, but not as you think.
However, it seems odd, her wings

let the rain roll across the perfect overlap
of her feathers. She's more like all
the chickadees, juncos, nuthatches,

finches that return to the feeders
hanging from the curly willow a few feet
from our front steps. They're all here

again today. Last night just before bed I
filled the feeder. Usually they empty it
in two, three days. It felt good—and right—

to fill those feeders. We were told
so many times this day would come.
Those who could have stopped it

didn't. The rain's become a gullet fall.
No wind. Another car has driven by. I'm glad
I have my coffee and a book inside to read.

Waiting for Covid

There are no daily warnings of the flu,
no curves, movements, annual data.
No news on Betty down a block or two. She

has the flu. "So, you had it too?" "I did,
felt awful; thought I'd die. Then today I
wake up fine, even shoveled our walk."

I was four when I got pneumonia,
couldn't leave the house for seven months.
Some days my mother brought me breakfast.

I had puppets, toys, and Gram who read me
comics: *Bugs and Porky, Hopalong Cassidy,*
Tarzan, Little Lulu. My bed became a spaceship

hurtling to Jupiter, Venus, Mars. I could escape
the twelve-eyed aliens whose longer than light
years poisons sent me steering across the airless

atmosphere. Then my unanticipated cough blew
them into galactic dust. I'd drift deep into the
timelessness of sleep and in the morning land

awake, Gram welcoming me home. Now
I wait, wear a mask, hope the vaccination holds.
Grieve.

What If

1

My father, born a hunky, bore
the sneer and slander slung
at those who lugged names
holding three times as many
consonants as vowels.
His job: to drag the family
from the soot-shadowed
hardscrabble Pittsburgh mills.
He grew up on Goat Shit Hill
where at the street's top end
his father cemented a hoop
and demanded that he learn
to shoot the only thoughtful way.
He'd obey or the family's disrespected
ball would ricochet and roll
a long and lonely mile
away from his family's
only hope. He was the first
to leave: go to college, go
to war where once again a captain—
his company Black—he argued
locked white minds for equal shoes,
weapons, helmets, rain gear
so they could slog through mud and wreckage
across Europe and the Philippine swamps.
He believed the war would never end.

2

In the early 50s, I sat with him
at basketball games. Partway
through one game he wondered, What if

17

no one plays a set position? What if
no guard has to stay in place, no
forward, not the center even? What if
every player's moving all the time,
plays anywhere? What if
everyone's in motion?

3

It's 1959. It's the semi-final for
the national championship. He's
playing Tennessee A&I, three
straight national champs, a team
that took a score usually ending
in the 50s, maybe 60s, into a torrid
pace and race to 90, 100. Dad's team
was down one. He looked at the clock.
Three minutes left.
He called time out.
He locked his eyes
on each player, then calmly said,
"Hold onto the ball for the last shot."
Each eye widened. "Three minutes?!"
"Yeah."
"We're behind!"
"That's right."

4

In the 70s, he thought, What if
we don't play man to man or
zone? What if we don't guard
anyone? What if we interrupt
the passing lanes? They tried
it at Virginia, won by 20, and
after the game the press asked

coach Terry Holland, "What
the hell happened out there?"
The coach shrugged, said,
"Damned if I know. It was like
we were playing against an amoeba."

5

Go back to 1958, back, back
before Kentucky/Texas Western,
back before civil rights became
a centerpiece of consciousness.
My father tells my mother,
"I'm gonna start Chuckie, Nick,
and Ron." Three Black, two white.
They won by twenty-five.
The next morning came a call:
"The president requests you
see him in his office, ten-thirty.
Be on time. He has a meeting
at eleven." Dad came home
for lunch. We sat together
with our bologna sandwiches
and carrot sticks. My mother,
tight-lipped and tilting her head
asked, "What did the president
want?" My father frowned, said,
"He told me he got calls.
Then he stared at me.
You know his eyes. He stared
and, you know that growl,
ordered, 'Next game you will
play,' then held up and pushed
two fingers at me." We sat still
silent, scared. We had

a house, a car, these sandwiches
because he coached. I took a breath
and stammered, "Next game?
What are you gonna do?"
My father looked at each
of us, then said,
"Next game," and
slowly raised four fingers.

   –for my father

Across the Room

In a fading photograph sitting on a
wobbly end table, my great-grandfather
holds the reins of two slow-hoofed horses

draped in bells. He drives a beer wagon,
barrels of pilsner and lager brewed nine miles
from this very corner on a Pittsburgh twisting

hillside. For me there is no photograph. He's
still driving the wagon, softly calling to Jess and
Josh who know only work and a bed of straw,

two roans who once gave rides in a carnival
that carried each town's loneliness back and forth
over the Ohio River for five years, letting anyone ride:

child, grandmother, tall, short, first timer,
a lying cowboy who had ridden nothing more
than an old St. Louis bar stool. Now across

the long lost trail of memory's belief he
sits, the devotion of his dog beside him looking
one way as he looks long down the other.

II.

ONE CHILDHOOD

Let Us Break Bread Together on Our Knees

And the angel said unto thee, Go thou
into your garden and plant creeping Jenny,
alyssum, sweet woodruff to crawl across

the earth, and herbs to bring culinary alchemy
into each and every meal: oregano, rosemary,
lemon balm, chives, sage, and thyme. Then

set deep into the soil two wisteria vines, three
redbud trees, a butterfly bush, lupines, salvia,
zinnias—a hundred zinnias. Wait for the bees.

Wait for the 20,000 kinds of bees, from bumble
to honey to mason. Watch how they live in
harmony, all humming as if they can trust

one another and the petals, stamens, the ways
the flowers make their indifferent offerings
of pollen. Be ever humble in your unknowing.

Learn the intelligence of worm, vole, sparrow,
spider, how none needs even a holy word
to linger and work, becoming nothing more

than what they are, under the benign disregard
of sky, the unpredictable nonchalance of weather.
Genuflect to the bees that ye may eat of the fruit of the land.

It's Always Within the Wood

He's sanding down
a branch he's taken
from under the trees
behind their house. He'll
sit here until noon, the air
taking the wood's slow dust.

In the afternoon, he'll take
his knife and start
to shave closer, circling
any knot, letting the grain
tell him where to go, letting
the shape arrive. Sometimes
a bird appears, sometimes
the moon, a boat, one time
a hand, often only the smooth
world of curve and edge.
He knows when his hands say no.

I Thought About Putting Together A Jig-Saw Puzzle

It's raining, a soft rain, not hard enough to bend
the coneflowers, pansies, and the spindly stems
of astilbe. Vivian, our dog, sleeps on the hardwood

floor, now and then letting out a snort and snore
always making me smile. Across the room,
my wife pedals her spinning wheel. Our mottled

gray cat ambles into the room, stops by Vivian,
rubs against her, lets her sleep, walks on
to hide and sleep herself behind the shirts hanging

from the low bar in the closet. This is one
understanding of time, a way to believe it
exists. Here we spend our days sitting in

the nothing that is never empty, that fills
with whatever comes along. How long
can we wait? Can we ask? Here is where

we live, where we wonder how Vivian lives
in a world with no need of forgiveness. She
knows nothing else, tail wagging after being

left alone with nothing to do. Her long day's
sleep a comfort? She makes her way
from floor to bed to couch carrying her stuffed and

soggy sloth. My wife is spinning wool from a fleece
she's cleaned, dried, dyed, combed and carded, evolving
it into yarn. Later she'll sit across from me and knit,

creating our quiet. We want to be as wordless as Vivian.

How We Must Waken

I was at the back window watching
   our dog, my wife, and our daughter,
      the dog bounding into the wind-drifted

snow as they, bundled and laughing,
   trudged their way to the front door.
      Jim Harrison reminds it's better to

live a sentimentalist than die a smart ass.
   The ornaments are still on the tree.
      We're still playing Irish carols.

It's a new year. But is there such a thing?
   The sun sets, rises, sets, and we name
      the days that tumble one into

another while 500 million light years away
   lies a galaxy with suns that have no
      days, no war, no need for a manger.

Here we must waken, roll away the stone
   from our empty tomb of sleep, step
      through another sunlit tragic day, trying

to believe in the snowplow, the mail,
   the hello from the next-door neighbor, the mourning
      doves fluffed at the nearly empty feeder.

Mid-Morning

Do you know what today is? It's another
day a lot like yesterday only we are
a lot older than we were yesterday. I bet

you didn't even notice. I know my day
was about the same. Maybe yours was like
this too. Awoke to the jazz station, peed.

Turned on the hot water pot, ground
the coffee. When the water boiled, I
poured it over the grounds, warmed

our cups, took my meds, made the bed,
fed the dog, the cat, brushed my teeth,
took off and folded my pajamas, got dressed,

put on a soft, comforting shirt and jeans. Did
I mention there is a pandemic? Of course
you know that. Why would I need to remind you?

That was certainly the same as yesterday. Even
if you had tea instead of coffee, we have the virus
haunting us in common. Purell in every room.

All these messages cheering us up. I sure don't need
to be cheered up. And how is being despairing keeping
the damn thing at bay? I prefer being neither despairing

nor cheerful. They swim together in my DNA. I'll tell you
what I do need: that cup of hot coffee, black, and the bed
pillows fluffed and ready. My plans for the day:
Listen to jazz and hope to make it back to that made bed.

One Childhood

Maybe that hesitation
just before I crossed
the street brought
the old woman to
the window. She
looked out, the way
a monk looks into
a prayer, then turned
and disappeared
into the dark of her
living room. That's
when I crept into
her yard, touched
the gray-green bark
on the old elm draping
itself across her porch,
then ran down into
the ravine behind her
gardens, knowing she
could rise up through
the chimney, float
down, point, and
turn me into a yellow
cat sitting on the front
porch rail, or into
a star hanging in
the night. The door
opened, and I heard
her call for her father.
I felt anonymous as
any stone, and knew
that even witches
carry what we carry.

Once It Happens

The moon, full and
rising at the end
of the boulevard

sat enormous
over the cross street,
over the little park

with its seesaw,
slide, three swings,
two weathered benches,

and a sandbox. Our
daughter, two years old,
was toddling down

the cracked and
crooked sidewalk,
arm outstretched,

finger pointing.
I'd allowed her
to wobble ahead,

but then the father
in me realized she
wasn't going to stop.

Quiet as a prowler,
I stiffened myself
to break into her

separate world,
quickened my walk,
and within my silence,

a step or two behind,
heard her chanting
as if in prayer,

"Touch moon. Touch moon."

Clothespins

Go back to the world where clothes hung to dry
on a long line in a breeze, the wind, or daylong

sunlight in the steadied air. Clothespins held
like our lips when we backseat sat at the drive-in

never knowing one day it would be an antique,
even a ruin one might see on a back road behind

a town too small to tear it down. Once after
thirty-some years together, we made popcorn,

put a couple Cokes in a cold pack and parked
at the drive-in just outside our village,

next to a speaker dangling from its rusting perch,
placed it on the window rolled halfway down

and stared at the abundance of white screen.
Our marriage was playing, a double bill with

all that came before. I said, "You remember
clotheslines. And clothespins." "Of course."

And we remembered Mondays, how we would
see at almost every house, a line and the pins

holding fast the sheets, pillow cases, shirts and bras,
blouses, jockey shorts, and socks, even dish towels,

each in the universe of air, then we opened the Cokes, raised
them, kissed as tight as clothespins, and watched the show.

Bartholomew: Disciple

He would say, "Follow," and we would.
One word; his word and we were
turned into fools, letting him take us
all that way. Why we did, to this day
I don't know. Look how it ended. Look
what it became. What did we have
to stay for? Nothing. There wasn't much
to do. The poor were everywhere.
We ate mostly bread and fish. We heard
story after story and, well, look it up.

In the big deal painting, I'm rather
glassy-eyed, and it wasn't the wine.
Miracles? They had been going on before.
But I will say it was his words. Words!
Words had never done what his did.
I'd listen. Later I would try to make sense
of them. I never could. But I could feel them.
Maybe that was it, how they got inside you,
made you wonder and wrinkle. He reversed
things, the first shall be last; the last first.
Everything changed.

I started looking at lepers and the poor and paid
no attention anymore to the kings and scribes and
Pharisees. I had thought the world of them. Now
their importance felt unimportant. You started seeing
everything within a new mind. You were drawn into
a new world, a world spinning within a world, one
drawing you in, while the old one imposed itself
on you. The reversals made me want to plant
what hadn't belonged—Lilies in wheat fields.

You couldn't say, "So what!" Words really
became flesh. And my flesh held a kingdom.
Now most everything I believed didn't matter.
Reason sure didn't. And money, and go make
your list. Every single day we'd head off, follow,
always wondering what we'd eat and where
we'd sleep. Our feet were filthy. My god, we
were always filthy. We stank. And then he'd
point at birds or stalks of grain, even stop and
have us kneel before a flower. Then he'd smile.
That haunts me still. That smile. And then he died.
They killed him. Love? He brought out their hate.
He had a terrifying sense of mercy. Nothing he said or loved

was impossible. Maybe that was it. It all seemed possible.

A Perfect Day for a Ballgame

All we had was the open field Johnny
mowed. We said he could play if
he cut it short. It was Saturday.
Enough of us from our little town

could make up two teams. We had no
mound. Lou and Kenny alternated choices,
Kenny first, his hand last climbing the bat.
Of course Johnny, the only one left,

played right field. Each pitcher tossed it in
easy, letting us hit, giving the defense plenty
to do. We spiked down three ragged T-shirts
for bases; home plate a slab of plywood Sam

brought from his father's lumberyard scrap.
We loved playing with no one watching.
And no umps. We'd alternate arguments
over every close play. Billy wanted to bloody

Ziggy's nose, then caught himself with, "Yeah,
okay, your call." We played till dark, got home,
sat by ourselves with a cold dinner. Smiled.
Why in the world would we care? We had our

gloves, nearly round balls, hero-inscribed bats,
caps, brims curved into half moons. The scores
were 9-4, 16-13, 11-9. That wasn't what mattered.
Four guys homered. There were maybe nine errors.

Who's counting? But we'll remember that one
double play, as fine as Tinker to Evers to Chance,
Evers making a leaping turn and toss. Even Johnny
forgot he was chosen last. Best ball he ever played.

–for Sue Oestreich

On Certain Nights

The cats climb down
off their porches and
skulk behind the empty

houses. The Presbyterian
minister kisses his wife
good night and works

until early morning on
his sermon as the moon
creases the space above

the quiet single street.
Everyone knows it's
time for the gardeners

to sleep, for the widows
to dream their husbands
back in new suits.

Because of William Stafford

I walked to the river.
It didn't say a word.
I walked into the river.
It moved on by.

I walked to the old oak.
It didn't say a word.
I sat under its old branches.
The leaves fell around me.

I walked to the robin's nest.
It didn't say a word.
I watched the mother fly to a nearby branch.
Small heads rose.

I walked through the meadow.
It didn't say a word.
I stood amid the wildflowers.
They waved in the wind.

I walked in the wind.
It never said a word.
I felt it cross my face.
It was gone and there and gone.

III.

THE LOST SIMILES

The New Normal

At home the prosthetic lay on the top
shelf of his closet. They told him it

would be like everything was normal
again. He'd walk just the same. Some day

he would even run. He looked at them.
Never went to rehab. Once he was home

he never put it on. Up to the very top
shelf it went. "Normal," he told

her, "is a word like 'real world.'
This, this is normal, here, where I

had a leg. That's normal." She pictured
the minefield. "Next they'll say, 'You

can return to normal.' Where was I?
Sleeping by you with one leg,

that's returning to normal." She looked down.
"That phony leg gonna help the kids,

keep them both normal?" It was snowing.
He grabbed his crutch. "I'm goin' out,

walk in the woods." "I'll go with you.
Want me to go with you?" "No. I'll be gone

just a little while. Walking in the snow will
seem normal." He made his way out the back

door, the snow falling harder, faster. He paused
by an old maple, looked down, saw the edge

of the blanket they took to games, pulled it out.

"If It Didn't Exist, I Wouldn't Miss It"

–Our daughter when asked about fourth grade math

But of course it's there. Along with scrambled
eggs. And all these books, and the recordings

left from when I had no idea they didn't matter,
didn't until I gave them to the kid next door

who had moved here from Iowa, and nothing
against Iowa which I have never been to

which I guess means I don't care if Iowa exists.
Now as for me, I loved math as long as I didn't

have to have the right answer. Don't you love
a 2? Especially a 2. I myself can't have

enough of them: their beautiful curves.
Formulas were cool. All those lines

and combinations of shapes and signs.
Just leave off the answers. Another thing

I wouldn't miss—answers. Answers
can't be lost, even hidden in a simile.

–for Jim Allis

After Reading the Table of Contents of Three Literary Magazines and Recognizing Two Names

Galway! When did this happen? Adrienne? Bill?
Charles? Etheridge, Nancy, Jane, Jerry, Lucille?

We'd hang out together whether or not we knew
one another's home address or sent each other

holiday cards. I was never on the cover
but sometimes got to be there on page

14 or 82 or 20. Now when I walk into
a conversation, ready with my questions

for these new kids on the page about family
and what they're working on, I overhear

adamant stances on the quaint oppression
of alliteration, the sentimentality of caring,

that assonance is oh so old school. I want
to shout, "News from the heart!" Instead I'll

walk to work with Wallace, make a house call
on a back street with W.C., then invite

W.S. and Conrad over for coffee and glazed donuts,
no longer caring if icing's clinging to my beard.

My Mother's Ivory Hippopotamus

It's the opening of April and no
month is cruel. The robins are back,
fat and cold. Some days, the slow

silent float of snow, the irredeemable
clatter of sleet, hail hurling against
the windows, then finally the arrival

of first rain, permissions to be alone
with some piano jazz, a photo album,
stiff drink, even a drowsy conversation

with oneself. Someone is praying. Here
we're merely hoping no one calls, our cats
happy sitting together on the windowsill.

What lies ahead is day after day. What
spreads out behind doesn't matter any
more. The night will drape itself across

our dwindling, the moon still giving itself
to the myth of moonlight. Time hides
within the jazz notes hallucinating into

what we hear. On a shelf between family
photographs, my mother's ivory hippopotamus.
Tomorrow, I'll leave it there again.

Saint Mark and His Piano

He could feel his fingers widen with harmony,
counterpointing the sacred implications
of the secular, the riffs of faith, the classical

intonations of jazz. They are always there
from thumb to the stretch of the little finger:
Benny Green and Bach, Horace Silver

and Liszt, Dave Brubeck and Chopin.
Later when he took the walk he'd almost
forgotten, along the usual path, he watched

the sun, knew the way the light keeps opening
the spaces between the leaves, brings dust
into a dance as each foot moves on then

settles. At one point he stopped his stroll
and waited for his trained eyes to open, trying
again to understand why each stem bordering

his prayer-withheld path holds on and up, how
even trees split by lightning branch and branch
again, and he feels time in his blood and wonders

in worry why what he'd written is being read.
He remembers no one healed, no risen dead,
sees no twitch of change in the twisted lineage

of Pharisee. God is still. Ineffably unable. Yet
there are emptied followers, and in their shabby
and dismembered world he plays his piano, wants

to believe they hear the silences between the notes.

Have You Had Your Vaccine?

Yeah. You? Yeah, had both. Well, then let's
hang out. We can wear masks to be safe.

Great! We'll get the old way back. Don't
bring anything. We have so much beer. I

keep buying for people coming by. We've
been lucky. What we love we've not had

to give up. I tell you, we readers win in the end.
My father'd order me, "Put down that book. Do

some work around here!" I would. Anyway,
how about Friday around two-three o'clock? Perfect.

You have ants? Not too many. I take it you do.
Oh god, yeah. Everywhere. Thought I could

get rid of 'em with those little round container things.
But oh no. I guess some got out fast enough to tell

the others to get the hell away from there. Guess
so. How about the Pirates? Who would have ever thought

they'd be playing five hundred ball, even in the spring?
Yeah, the god of baseball works in mysterious ways.

Pretty soon they'll get back to losing. Think so?
I wonder. My kid started to shave. Now he hardly

ever looks at us. The other night we're having a good
dinner, and he says he doesn't like peas anymore.

I said, Peas? Peas are good for you, for your eyes.
Center fielder needs good eyes, and at bat he'll never detect

the curve without a good eye. Yeah, it's like last week
we went to the mall and all our kid said was No to

every cool pair of pants we liked. We came home with light brown jeans, light brown. Kinda tan. Not light blue

even. Light brown. I don't get it. He never does anything all that wrong. He's a good kid. But light brown jeans?

Did he look good in 'em? I guess so. I saw others in 'em. How on God's green earth would someone like me know?

Maybe Tomorrow

He drove across the center
line, hit her head on. Turned her
into a quadriplegic. He was

eighteen. It doesn't matter.
She's seventy. Her eyes wouldn't
open. The sun was bright, a cloud-free

day, the sky blue as the blue one can't
explain or describe. If you woke into
such a day you would think nothing

could go wrong. Our daughter, when
she enters her art room, alchemizes
school into a studio. Do we need

to know why he crossed the line?
What he was thinking or doing, not
doing? He died. They pried

her free. The surgeons assure everyone
she will live. But for what? Tomorrow's nothing
but time. We send cards,

emails, texts, flowers, make
visits, make gifts. We hope her eyes
will find the window. We hope she'll

discover her own air to breathe.
Today we voted. The line wasn't long.
We were home for breakfast. Then

I walked our dog. The hospital bed
bends her up. Her brother and sisters
came, are standing at her side, stay

at her house with her cat, Pete.
Her church will place her on their
prayer list. Today I have yoga.

After that I'll do the laundry, do
the dishes, do what else needs to
be done. Then I'll check her

CarePages, leave another message,
say the same thing a different way.
Later, once again, I'll walk the dog,

then fill the bowl for our cats. It's
November. The leaves have let go.
Maybe tonight when I walk our dog

I'll be a kid kicking the leaves.

–for Marianna

The Man Who Loves Olives

Every day, he goes to the store
at the end of his street and buys
a jar of olives. He pretends
they are from the south of France,
grown by a family who first planted
the trees just after the Romans had
cleared out leaving the sun and the
light and the mistral. He imagines
the trees, twisted, full of gnarled
knots, rooted deeper than their
history. He knows how the branches,
even when broken, bent, cut back
to nothing but a sprig send
shoots back up into the hot, dry summer.
He knows how difficult it is to pick
a single olive, how they hold to the
tangle of branches, how the timing
has to be perfect or the lovely bitter
taste will fail. When he gets home,
he sits on his porch, twists off the lid,
picks out a single olive, black or green,
and drops it in his mouth, pausing,
letting the red clay in his imagination
open, letting the trees stand against
the wind. He bites down, smiles,
shudders, then pulls out another, the sun's
light coming through the screens,
the end of the day rising like his past.

–for Greg Rappleye, who loves olives, lots of olives

How It Should Be

It was on a Tuesday, or was it a Thursday?
What makes one wonder about a day
when the day doesn't much matter

outside of a crime scene? And this has nothing
whatsoever to do with a crime scene. It
has to do with Yo-Yo Ma playing Bach

again, and playing in such a way that Bach
wandered into the room with a silver tray that
held a plate of macaroons, a flowered pot of tea,

a bottle of bourbon. I swear I had fallen asleep,
dreaming. But no. I had begun writing this
and I am sure our dog had pushed her black

butt up against me the way she does to assure
us both that we are here together, safely
with one another, she softly feeling

my presence as she faces forward, able to be
awakened by the quietest of sounds, sounds
she's not heard before, and alert me with

her wary bark. I thanked Johann, took two macaroons,
placed them on a small china plate bordered by
twisting ivy—surely hand-painted—a linen napkin,

and slowly poured an inch and a half of bourbon, neat,
into a small but heavy glass. "Help yourself to as much
as you like," said Johann. And we listened together.

What? You Wouldn't Want to Be a Dog?

A loved dog? A cherished dog? A dog
sleeping on the couch, on the throw rug,

on the porch on a sunny summer day, on the back
seat on the way out west or to the pharmacy?

There's not much you'd need to do. Nothing
you'd have to buy. Breakfast: there. On time.

Dinner: there, though you may need to bark.
Snack? Sit. Or roll over. And they clean up.

Four walks a day, never caring if they
are bored by the same scenes. You're busy

smelling yourself into worlds they will never
know, worlds carried on the air, and always new.

Scents hidden under moldering leaves, along
a log composting itself into the earth: it's

an olfactory feast, a glory unknown to all
but dogs. And you are even welcomed to

an anus newly met—or a neighbor. You
don't have to vote. You don't have to keep up.

You don't need the latest pleated pants,
a pair of shoes to wear to church. Your

god is always there in every pat and scratch.
Not one worry about the economy, the weather,

getting a good night's sleep, the Iowa Caucus.
You never need to say a thing. You will never

know that anything will happen. You won't know
one day you won't be here. You will wag your tail.

The Lost Similes

Like the way the nuthatch comes down a tree headfirst

Like two vanilla wafers left on the platter

Like winter leaving behind ice by the road

Like your sister's hair when she was in seventh grade

Like a pair of shoes by the door

Like spring coming and going

Like a bucket of mulch sitting beside the bicycle

Like a rusted tire iron

Like butterbur spreading under the white pines

Like a grandmother's crooked smile

Like eleven days without going to the post office

Like that regret

Like when it rained all night and into the morning

Like nothing you know

IV.

SOME KID WAS SHOT

Just Before Spring

When you are this old, you have to
learn about the day every day,
as the water heats, create some kind of life

before you finish your morning coffee. There
was a time when all I knew how to do was play.
With the puppets: it was their world.

I could build a fort, sit there and feel its safety
for any loving length of time. I could play ball and
collect acorns in a tin box. Of course I could

do this now, do it all again. Jung did. But every
day it's the same chair waiting for when the dog
finds my lap. I wonder about last night, why

the wind brought rain from the north. I wonder
what lonely force brought hate, why now the sky
is cloud-empty. The only risk is a walk to town

to buy another cup of coffee, maybe this time
a latte. Maybe someone will be there who
has found a home in the past, one with toy trains,

Lincoln logs, maybe a town built of cardboard
where your sixth grade shyness lived, and the girl
who smiled at you every day moved next door.

On the Inhumane Hideaway of
Objective Distance

My wife is at her spinning wheel. She
first cleans, dries, and combs the fleece,
then dyes the wool. She will spin yarn to make

a shawl, stocking cap, socks. She disappears
into her gentle quiet. I am a third of the way
through reading four books, but I don't want

to read any of them. I want what I know you
want: to be happy, actually happy, to love
in a happy world. Today there was yet another

school shooting. Some students felt it coming.
Three kids who thought they were grown up,
dead. One more, thought likely to die, did. The

others will live. The news dares to say "recover."
Tonight we played Christmas carols for the first
time this season. Yes, 'tis the season. This morning

surgeons at three different hospitals awakened
assuming yet another routine day of rounds and
operations. When they were seventeen, did they

imagine advent would offer them the inevitable
impossibility of saving the assumption of a future,
that they would never again be able to say, Happy

Holidays, Merry Christmas, Happy Hanukkah,
Happy New Year without being caught in an ambush
of memory? Tonight thousands of parents will be unable

to sleep, or tomorrow, or on into ever. Teachers
who each day hope it will not, cannot happen again
will think about construction jobs, or an office.

And guns? They will sleep in the garage, a cabinet,
on the top shelf. They will rest and be at the ready.
No, I don't want to read; I don't want to hear again

about God's mercy, the peace that comes from above
or meditation, Calvin's endlessly facile legacy of sin,
the need for prayer and legislation. I'm tired of pursuing

happiness. I want to breathe it in as ubiquitous as air.
And while we're at it, I want education revised
to teach the truth of sentimentality, that it's not any more

fake feeling than the unguarded synapses in the shooter's brain.
Scholars, put away the safety of your secondary sources. Sit
with your students. Abandon the inhumane hideaway of

objective distance. Throw open your hearts. Let sentiment
break any shielded soul before another rifle and a surgeon's
words do. My wife never asks for meaning. She sits

in silence at her wheel twisting a single lamb's
wool into yarn to knit what keeps another warm.
Our dog is asleep, head on her paws. The twin sister cats

curl together. I'm not going to pick up my books. I'm
going to begin to trim the tree wondering how many
five-year-olds will sit on Santa's lap and when he asks them,

"What do you want for Christmas?" will answer, "A gun."

The Night Before a Friend Had To Put Down Her Dog

I look across the living room, our dog, Vivian,
asleep, snoring and twitching on the sofa, her
head resting on two pillows she herself piled

one on the other. Outside, another winter
storm has laid its snow across the lawn, its
wind-borne white having fallen through

the woods behind our old house. Of course
it isn't our woods. And of course, neither is
the house nor Vivian ours. We own

nothing. Why, I wonder, can dogs be ever so
good to us? Ever welcoming, everything ever
new? Even on the same old walk four times a day.

I can just as well ask why the snow, the stars,
why raspberries, and certainly why us. My wife
endures my bewilderment as daily she spins wool

into yarn. I, in wasteful wonder, wonder how can
this possibly be? Her peddled, preserved way
of fleece to yarn and then to shawls, her gentle,

quiet, numinous, and nimble fingers ignoring
death at the door always offering one more
memory waking the unwelcome ache.

Death then turns, parting with "Be back soon."
I know I should stow the dishwasher, slide three
Robert Johnson CDs into the player. It will soon

come time to walk Vivian. She will sniff her way
along her olfactory trail. I, as still commanded
by my grandmother, will dress "warmly." For now

Vivian sits, waits, nose pressed against
the back door calmly urging me to go
into the accompaniment of cold, the snow

wind-cast and swirling around us, my
shoulders hunched, her nose plunging, happy.

Grief Again

"One of us is going to go through this again,"
she said. "If we marry," he said. "Even if we

don't," she said. "Or we could go together,"
he said. "You know, in a crash or double suicide."

And outside, in the garden they had grown
together, it was June and all but the fall

flowers had blossomed or bloomed. The
forsythia bushes bordering the back side

awaited bee-glazed pollen, and the lopsided
leaves of the hostas bent toward the compost

cultivated soil. They walked to the garden, sat on
their Adirondacks as the chickadees, house wrens,

finches, and nuthatches flew branch to branch to
the sunflower seed feeder. She reached across

the rotting arm of her chair, softly settling her hand
on his arm. He took a sip of cold, morning coffee.

The squirrels and chipmunks chased one another amid
the hollyhocks, impatiens, white roses, the morning glories.

–for Mary Toppen-Palma

Remember That Rock Song?

I seldom do. It's not that it's a wonder.
It's more a mystery, not like in the book

you read in bed, waking in the morning
with it open to the wrong page and lying

next to your pillow. It's a blue sky hanging
over the wire walker tip-toeing between

two high-rises. If you were there you would
look up pulsing your neck muscles and bewildered

by those who just walk by, even beneath, who pay
no mind, head on to what's waiting on the desk.

Perhaps they'll buy a morning paper, learn
that around 2am some kid was shot, killed.

That will be something to talk about. Did
he have it coming? The point being? The

wire walker sits down dead center, then stands,
prances to the wire's far end. The banks

have been open since 9 am. It's that time
of year when some people wonder if any

of this is worth it. Some stay alive. After all, there
is so much to talk over once again. Along the shore

the waves break large or small.

Her Bed

During the worst of the storm, lightning
glazed the night's same sky, thunder loud
enough to keep her from hearing her sigh

as she tried again to stop imagining. Her cat
leaped onto the bed, crossed over the pillows
on the left side, then jumped back down onto

the uncarpeted oak floor over which on
moving day there had been rose-colored
tile, then dashed back to the sleep spot

in the clothes closet under his trousers
dangling to a half inch from the floor.
The crocuses were up and opening,

some yellow, almost gold, some reverently
purple. But a frost could lean them into
the mulch. The pandemic was over. But

a pandemic, as they said, may never
die. Another slash of lightning
split her window pane. She had spent

her day listening to her complete collection
of Dvořák. It, of course, took all day. She
had decided to read the background of each

piece. She paused once to call her sister,
but all she could think to say was "I am so glad
I know hardly a thing about music." Her

sister asked how she was so she said
she'd had two burritos for a late lunch.
"Funny: burritos and Dvořák. I want to listen

to some more now. Bye." It kept raining. It kept thundering. All afternoon. Into the evening. Her cat finally came out, went to his bowl for dinner.

She listened on as the sun set, then the cat again leaped onto the bed. She smiled, remembering how hard a time she'd had learning to ride a bicycle.

On the Bus to Poland

Where's Daddy?
I don't Know.
Tell me why you don't know.
I don't know why I don't know.
When will we know?
I don't know. I wish I did.
Does Daddy know where we are?
You mean on this bus?
Yes.
I think he does. I hope he does.
I'm hungry.
I know.
I'm thirsty, too.
I know.
Do we have anything?
We will later. I hope.
How much is later?
I don't know.
Where are we going?
A new country. Its name is Poland.
Is it like where we live?
Kind of.
Are the people like us?
I think so.
Are they nice?
I'm sure they must be.
Does Daddy know we're going there?
I think he does, yes.
Will my friends be there when we get there? I'm hungry.
I know you are.
My friends. Will they be there?
I don't know. That would be nice.

Did you bring Suzzy?
I did. Suzzy's in that big bag.
There are a lot of trees here.
Yes. There are.

He Had Put It Off For A Year

The trunk of the apple tree had rotted.
Any arborist would know why. Probably

any apple farmer. He knew a result
is not an explanation. Before I started

writing I couldn't know if this pen
would make its way to the period.

The apple tree had never moved.
It was after all an apple tree and

was now dying in late spring while
still offering bouquets of white blossoms.

He took down the saw from the shed
his father'd built from leftover lumber.

His grandfather had planted the tree.
He remembers climbing it, pretending

to be a raccoon peering down into the
ground cover of night. The tree now

leaned north, the lower branches brushing
the untrimmed grass. His wife stood

at the open front door. Their dog sat
beside him, tail wagging, and up through

the blossoms, an all but full moon rose,
a glimpse through the passing clouds.

Yesterday I Buried a Female Cardinal

Early this morning I sat by the window
watching the feeders: thistle for the

finches, sunflower seeds for the others,
watched within the rising light as one

after another the returning birds pecked
a seed, flew through the spring, sprouting

leaves deep into the woods where somewhere
nests seemed to rest as nearer and nearer came

time for the fledglings to raise their heads.
My wife was at her spinning wheel. Tonight

we will sit together in the room we call
The Cottage, reading. Cardinals mate

for life. Yesterday as I lay the female cardinal
beneath the sod and placed some pinched off

pansies over the soft mound, I noticed, several
trees away, a single male, its bright red a dissonance

to my burial. Later I would take on my morning
round of needs. But then I turned on the blues station,

sat at the window with my coffee, black. My wife
left her wheel, pulled a chair beside me. We stared

at the holly, coming coral bells and hyacinths
at the edge of the woods, then watched the common

red sitting where two trunks grew apart.

Light at the End of Day

She would wait each night until the sun lugged
its leftover light into its next awakening.

Then if the night were cloud-clear, she'd step
through the stone path in her garden, no

matter the season, sit on the moss-clothed
and weakening wooden love seat and

watch the stars. She did not believe in
the celestial celebrities, constellations

that had long lost meaning, sprawled
and appealing to those who wanted

to point them out and announce an investment
of learning to someone staring up and seeing

only what appeared to be salt spilled across
heaven's unnecessary table. No, she came out

ready to discover her own newly configured
constellations evoked by any collection

of the stars' singular light. She kept the
name in the blank book he'd given her.

After their anonymous parting she laid
a cut of twisted ivy on the first page

knowing each night there was no goodbye.

*–for Naomi Shihab Nye
and Rosemerry Wahtola Trommer*

There's Been a Suicide On This Page

He just couldn't
do the same thing
this morning. So he finished

his second cup,
of coffee with cream,
and quietly took his life.

His dog was asleep. His
cat was lying along
the window sill, watching

the snow fall and the birds
nudging through the wind
to the feeder he'd filled.

He had walked two miles
every morning after coffee,
skipped lunch, cooked dinner, and

other than on this page, slept well.

On Another Anniversary of My Father's Death

I hold a stone.
I ask it where
it's been, what
it's seen. And then
I listen. I spend
the morning listening
to the languages
within silence.
Above me on a branch
of a dying elm
a robin, just the usual
singular robin and
its irregular chirp.
I sit streamside,
the water moving
much like we do even
though we don't know our
creek beds and we tell
ourselves what we have
to do. The stone and I
no longer need each other.
We never did. I set it
on the water and watch
it settle beside the others.

V.

THE WORTH OF WAITING

Margaritaville Farewell

Put away your guitar. Let it
grieve beside you while Jimmy
smiles and charms a few chords,
two, three, four more than you're
ready for. It was that sane soul's
tone, man. That's what it was, that
softshell tone. Open the door, welcome
the sun to sit beside you. Just you and
the lonely old sun watching clouds
pass you by. Listen to how Jimmy
sang. Even moonlight bright
enough to keep you and the Captain
alive and wondering where that lover
is now. Sit and remember that night
you got drunk and stayed awake.
And that love, sleeping somewhere
outside Omaha, so you heard, never
gave you another thought. But Jimmy
didn't forget, and brings it back,
tells you to make a margarita or,
hell, anything to have your tears be
another thing to laugh about and then
toss overboard. Jimmy, you sang us
into a world we couldn't take the time
to make. So what if it wasn't possible?
We'll still carry every laid-back lyric
and the way it always should've been.

–with gratitude to Jimmy Buffett

After Leaving Bed at 2 AM I Wondered if I Was Still in the Same House

The leaves left on the trees will tear
like paper lanterns. The silverware
in the oak drawers has gathered old
notes along their handles. I sit down
into the overstuffed chair, the one
with the frayed brown arms and
the coffee stains, and pretend
there is a window beside me, that I
can see a weary cat sitting on a cell-twisted
branch of an elm. I wonder if I should
cut it down, make a space where
anything could appear: clover,
sandbox, a small town where the
mail carrier changes hats and drives
to a fire, later changes again and
walks along the cracked and peeling
downtown swinging the billy club
he used once to help Mrs. Keese
tap in a For Sale sign in front
of her four-bedroom house.

Nathaniel Before the Storm

When he said, "Follow me," I believed
something would make the sky cloudless
and blue as my wife's eyes, the eyes
of the woman I then left, she hoping,
standing over the fire, stirring the same
dinner. Our village had little to live for,
only prayer, a dozen huts, three with
children, all believing they needed
nothing more than the same two meals
blessed twice each day. And so it was
I trusted this man who, when saying, "Follow
me," would lead me somewhere, anywhere
that would let me return with what at last
would lighten the withering world
my wife had no way to rest within, tending
to "all that a woman was created for." Maybe
he knew of a place with fewer unexpected
days. Yes, I thought it worth what seemed
a chance. But now, tired, dirt hardening
in my hair, pores, and knuckles, and after
I've lost count how many days and nights
I have followed in nothing but wind and dust,
with nothing to eat unless out of pity, and then
more often than less often stale bread and rancid
fish, olives, sometimes a jug of wine, sleeping
together while feeling alone, most nights under
the star-pricked sky with the uneven lantern light
of the moon. When I hear, "Follow," or "Go into"
another rag strewn, leper laden, shrouded town, I
want more and even more want, every day want,
to say, "I'm turning my back. I'm going home."

At Home

The wind is moving across the dunes,
and the sun-alert afternoon glows.
We have settled here.
There are friends,
few enough to be friends.
What we know whispers
beneath the bed's crocheted
canopy, hanging above us
as if to bring us closer.
During the day we walk
around the house, see
out the window: money plant,
beeches clawing the dunes,
the hole under the neighbor's porch
where the cats hide, the firewood
stacked by the back door, one
chipmunk sitting on top, the car rusting.
We are alone.
That keeps most everything never
ours, helps us keep a kindly distance,
preserves our only chance.

Before What Came Before

We were living in an Irish cottage just outside
the village of Ballyvaughan, the only place where
when asked, I was able to say I was a poet.

But this is rapidly turning into an anecdote rather
than the famine house fifty some yards from
our peat heated, soup and soda bread stocked

home. I say home because I can write poems
knowing in my bloodstream here I am a tradesman.
The famine house has no roof or door, no windows.

It's inhabited by inedible weeds gnarled, clinging
to the stone walls, and usually by an east wind. Who
lived here 'til there was nothing left but leaving?

I stand in what was a room where the children woke
from their one bed, starvation sleeping in every stomach.
Try wakening to a bird you've never needed to kill,

drinking hot water while washing mud from the knees
of each pair of pants, watching the children turning
into bone carrying insipid air, their mother silently

pleading to take them where they could emerge from
childhood. He would hold his hoe, one more day, each
day being the day before the next. But the hoe could only

drop into the malnourished earth, as impoverished as every spirit
bludgeoned into what was now a haggard search for a mere
dozen spuds, ten to the monarchy. When he turned in the ten

he could feel the knife blade against his thigh. Tonight
after dinner we will settle in with our books, our games,
feel cozy by the peat fire, have scones and tea while

listening to the rain against the windows, dappling the roof.

The One Note

After sleeping in Itzhak Perlman's bed,
I went out and bought a violin, placed it
under my chin, and stood there, bow in hand.
I learned to play one note, practicing it
for an hour every day for two months,
disciplining my fingers, like getting a dog
to sit without a thought. I would ever so
precisely draw the bow across the strings
listening for that one note on a recording by
Perlman of a Brahms or Adams symphony.
The note was loneliness, ethereal, common.
I loved feeling it hover over every day.
I knew it would be with me, from
then to when. After the sound appeared,
I disappeared, only this note
taking my place, alchemizing me into
a smile or sigh. And it's been so ever
since that night, sleeping head soft on his pillow.
This one note, played as
perfectly as any ever has,
welcomes me to sit with Mahler,
Sondheim, Shostakovich, Berlioz, Dvořák,
that note in their every composition.
Just as the mute stars each night give in
to their lost way, I now sleep on my pillow,
hoping always for one more day, bow in hand,
sought by each new composer in our time . . .

High Fly: The Outfielder

You wait. You look up, staring,
hoping you are in the unpredictable
spot, glove open, eyes open, the ball high
against a passing cloud you hope will hold
your perception steady, accurate as the slight
breeze counterpointing the dropping trajectory.
Should the cloud pass, the sky will deepen
blue and the ball without a backdrop will
turn your eyes cataract and into an empty
prayer. All that will be left is an ambush of
anxiety, and a lonely hope that every other eye does
not see you, now a beggar, holding open your glove.

The Hidden Permutations of Love

I thought I would build a fence.
Not to keep anything out or in.
I'd make it of stones and branches
piled in the woods out back. I'd
weave the branches. I'd balance

the stones, make the fence
a mixed reminder, two textures,
one holding me to the ground,
one taking me into what
is above. I would sit by

the window and watch her walk
along it, touching the wood and
stone. She would stop to notice
how I had finely fit each rock
and branch, the wind still able to move

through each open space. A sparrow
would come, perch long enough
to open a seed. Squirrels would
run along the ridge. I thought
I would plant English ivy, burning

bush, and wedding veil hoping
to see them climb, spread,
entangle, bring out the unnamable
greens of green, see them catch
the light, glisten in the rain.

–for Michael Delp and Jack Driscoll

The Worth of Waiting

Here in the time between snow
and the bud of the rhododendron,
we watch the robins, look into

the gray, and narrow our view
to the patches of wild grasses
coming green. The pile of ashes

in the fireplace, haphazard sticks
on the paths and gardens, leaves
tangled in the ivy and periwinkle

lie in wait against our will. This
drawing near of renewal, of stems
and blossoms, the hesitant return

of the anarchy of mud and seed
says *not yet* to the blood's crawl,
when the deer along the stream

look back at us, we know again
we've left them. We pull
a blanket over us when we sleep.

As if living in a prayer, we try
to Amen the late arrival of red,
the stun of green, the muted yellow

at the end of every twig. We will
lift up our eyes unto the trees hoping
to discover a gnarled nest within

the branches' negative space. And
we will watch for a fox sparrow
rustling in the dead leaves underneath.

All I Know Is It Was Dark

And we were walking in the snow, in the four
feet of snow that each winter piles up
along the east side of the house, the flakes
having been blown off the lake, off the roofs,
and into drifts higher than any stocking cap
you had knitted and I had on. Remember? Maybe?
We held hands, well actually gloves.
Well, I wore gloves. You had on mittens,
ones you had knitted. When you knit,
we rest on my grandmother's daybed,
the one as a child I pretended was a bus I drove
every day from the suburbs into the heart of downtown
Pittsburgh after the gray smoke had metamorphosed white.
I didn't know what "The Renaissance City" meant. I knew
only that each day Mrs. Schnelker pulled the cord to be left
off at Seventh Avenue. Today you are knitting and I am lying
on the daybed, feet on your lap. I keep things clean
where you comb a dry fleece, then you pull the wool, set up
your wheel, and spin. That night when we trudged through
the snowfall, glove around mitten, then mitten around glove,
one of us lost our balance. But the other held on.

Acknowledgements

Special thanks . . .

To each of you who have brought kindness into my days.

To those at CavanKerry Press—Joan, Tamara, Dana, Gabriel, and Dimitri—for saying yes and believing, and bringing me joy.

To Baron Wormser who transformed a scattershot of poems into a book.

To Jennifer Lee, Bridget Reaume, and Joy Arbor for your extraordinary copy editing and proofreading.

To all of you who created a teacher.

To Diane Seuss, Rosemerry Wahtola Trommer, James Crews, and Li-Young Lee for your humbling affirmations.

To Jane Harrington Bach, D.L. James, Todd Davis, Charlie and Judith Brice, Dan Gerber, Donald Revell, Chris Rhein, D.R. James, Carrie Newcomer, Greg Rappleye, Michael Delp, Mary Ruefle, Jim Lavilla-Havelin, Chris Siems, Norbert Kraas, Caprice Garvin, Mark Hillringhouse, Renee Waddell, Gary and Michele Gildner, Linda Nemec Foster, and Bob Hicok whose gifts to this heart kept it going to the page.

To the editors of the following for welcoming many of these poems to their world, some in a different form: *Aethlon; Busy Griefs, Raw Towns* edited by GF Korreck; *Colorado Review; Crosswinds; Dunes Review; Gatherings* edited by Phyllis Cole-Dai; *Good River Review; Image; I-70 Review; The; Listening*

Eye; The Louisville Review; Mockingheart Review; Paintbrush; Paterson Literary Review; Plainsongs; Poetry East; Poet Lore; Rattle, Poets Respond; The Reformed Journal; San Pedro River Review; Sport Literate; Talking River Review; Third Wednesday; Twickenham Notes; Waymark

And to each of you who read with an open heart.

CavanKerry's Mission

A not-for-profit literary press serving art and community, CavanKerry is committed to expanding the reach of poetry and other fine literature to a general readership by publishing works that explore the emotional and psychological landscapes of everyday life, and to bringing that art to the underserved where they live, work, and receive services.

Other Books in the Notable Voices Series

Glitter Road, by January Gill O'Neil
Deep Are These Distances Between Us, Susan Atefat-Peckham
The History Hotel, Baron Wormser
Dialect of Distant Harbors, Dipika Mukherjee
The Snow's Wife, Frannie Lindsay
Eleanor, Gray Jacobik
Without My Asking, Robert Cording
Miss August, Nin Andrews
A Car Stops and a Door Opens, Christopher Bursk
Letters from Limbo, Jeanne Marie Beaumont
Tornadoesque, Donald Platt
Only So Far, Robert Cording
Unidentified Sighing Objects, Baron Wormser
How They Fell, Annie Boutelle
The Bar of the Flattened Heart, David Keller
Same Old Story, Dawn Potter
The Laundress Catches Her Breath, Paola Corso
American Rhapsody, Carole Stone
Impenitent Notes, Baron Wormser
Walking with Ruskin, Robert Cording
Divina Is Divina, Jack Wiler
How the Crimes Happened, Dawn Potter
Descent, John Haines
Southern Comfort, Nin Andrews
Losing Season, Jack Ridl
Without Wings, Laurie Lamon

An Apron Full of Beans: New and Selected Poems, Sam Cornish
The Poetry Life: Ten Stories, Baron Wormser
BEAR, Karen Chase
Fun Being Me, Jack Wiler
Common Life, Robert Cording
The Origins of Tragedy & Other Poems, Kenneth Rosen
Apparition Hill, Mary Ruefle
Against Consolation, Robert Cording

All At Once was typeset in FF Tisa, a softer, more dynamic version of a nineteenth-century slab serif wood type. It was designed by Mitja Miklavčič for FontFont in 2008.